UNDERSTANDING RESILIENCE

Martina E. Faulkner MSW

INSPIREBYTES OMNI MEDIA

This publication is published and distributed worldwide in the English language in the following formats:

ISBN Paperback: 978-1-953445-80-3
ISBN E-Book: 978-1-953445-81-0

This book was printed in a manner that minimizes its impact on the planet and the environment. Learn more at: www.inspirebytes.com/why-we-publish-differently/

INSPIREBYTES OMNI MEDIA

Inspirebytes Omni Media LLC
PO Box 988
Wilmette, IL 60091

For more information, please visit www.inspirebytes.com
Graphics and photos: Canva Design Pro

HUMAN AUTHORED™
AG THE Authors Guild
4507644

"Fear has been given a bad rep. It isn't something to be avoided; rather, it is our life's mission. It's our duty to overcome our fears, whatever they may be. ...

It is up to us to accept our own powers and make up our own minds, and not leave it to someone else."

– Levison Wood –

Contents

"Out of suffering have emerged the strongest souls; the most massive characters are seared with scars."

— Khalil Gibran —

Introduction

How do you define resilience? Some might say it's about strength, while others could argue that it's more about flexibility. We can identify it when we see it in others, and we also may know what it feels like for ourselves. There are times when we can see resilience as a kind of softness in the midst of brutality, or as a firmness when things are poorly-defined. Interestingly, we are also able to recognize when we see someone who isn't being resilient.

However, even with all this knowledge and understanding, it's still not always easy to define when someone asks you what it is. Let's look at Merriam-Webster, which gives us two definitions:

1. The capability of a strained body to recover its size and shape after deformation caused especially by compressive stress
2. An ability to recover from or adjust easily to misfortune or change

As humans, it's the second entry that matters most, and it's easy enough to understand. So, why can it feel so hard to apply? Even though resilience might be easy to identify, it's hard for us to define because it can be expressed in so many unique ways. We know it when we see it and often put it on a pedestal—it's something to strive toward. And yet, there is no specific way to actually achieve it.

So, what is resilience, and perhaps more importantly, how do we create it?

What Is Resilience?

"Resilience is knowing that you are the only one that has the power and the responsibility to pick yourself up."

– Mary Holloway –

Simply stated: Resilience is an outward expression of inner growth. It's a state of being that is the result of showing up repeatedly and consistently over time. When we show up for ourselves and actually do the work we need to do to grow and evolve, we build a few byproducts, one of which is resilience. This, in turn, allows us to find a core stability that we can draw on when things become challenging.

Resilience Is A Byproduct

As a byproduct of other endeavors, you can't set out with a specific goal to cultivate resilience. This means that when you make the decision to work on yourself in a way that supports your inner growth (mentally, emotionally, and spiritually), you are building resilience at the same time. In that regard, resilience is a positive side effect of making decisions to work on yourself and your soul's progression. In the same way that physically working out your body can create muscle memory alongside strength, working on your inner world can create resilience alongside healing.

So, if resilience is the outward expression of the inner work, this also means that it is the result of the soul working in conjunction with the body, mind, and emotions. Therefore, it's multi-faceted in how it can serve you as you continue to move forward through life. This is why it can show up in so many different ways, from strength to flexibility, from softness to firmness.

> *"Like tiny seeds with potent power to push through tough ground and become mighty trees, we hold innate reserves of unimaginable strength. We are resilient."*
>
> — Catherine DeVrye —

It's also why we can so easily identify it when we see it happening in front of us, and why we can call things out that are supposed to look like resilience, but aren't. For example, when someone is showing strength by overcompensating. In pop culture, we sometimes call it the "Napoleon complex" or the "B.M.O.C" (Big Man On Campus) trope. This form of strength is a display, which makes it performative; it's not, therefore, actual strength... or resilience.

Resilience Is Not A Shield

Since strength is one of the ways we interpret or experience resilience, it can sometimes be used incorrectly in an attempt to be resilient, when what's really happening is anything but. Brute force is not resilience. True resilience is not a shield. To think that is a common mistake, and one that needs to be redirected.

When someone puts emotional armor on to protect themselves from others, this is not a form of resilience. Since resilience is the result of doing inner work, true resilience comes from the inside, not from the outside. Shields and armor are based in force, and force is often based in some measure of fear. Resilience, on the other hand, is rooted in truth, growth, and understanding.

To understand resilience, is to know <u>who</u> you are as well as <u>why</u> you are.

Why do you show up for things, or not? What makes you feel more engaged, or more invested and passionate? Yes, it's true that resilience creates a form of protection, but it's not a layer on the outside that you need strength to uphold; it's a resource on the inside that requires no strength from you, only alignment.

Resilience, therefore, is both a state of mind and a state of being. It is a presence as well as knowledge. When you have done the work on emotional, mental, and spiritual levels, your mind is able to bring all those pieces together into the present moment in new ways.

If you then add a physical layer to it, you can truly stand in your boots and feel rooted in who you are. This also means that resilience is about being who you are, and no longer feeling compelled to chase different definitions of yourself.

"When we learn how to become resilient, we learn how to embrace the beautifully broad spectrum of the human experience."

– Jaeda Dewalt –

© 2025 Martina E. Faulkner

When you build resilience, you shift how you show up in life. You could say that resilience gives you a new user's manual to life. In that way, it is similar to the tools in your mental-emotional toolbox, but it's not an actual tool because it's not something you can go out and acquire or achieve.

> "It is really wonderful how much resilience there is in human nature. Let any obstructing cause, no matter what, be removed in any way, even by death, and we fly back to first principles of hope and enjoyment."
>
> — Bram Stoker —

Acquiring resilience is a process and it takes time. It also takes consistency and a willingness to change. When you continually choose to show up for yourself, you will build resilience.

Doing Due Diligence

"Do not judge me by my success, judge me by how many times I fell down and got back up again."

— Nelson Mandela —

Even though resilience is not something you can specifically set out to learn, there are pieces that you can learn—that you must learn, actually—in order to build resilience. Most importantly, you will need a mindset shift. So, in order to achieve a shift in your thinking, you have to engage in some due diligence.

What Is Due Diligence?

Due diligence is most often associated with business and law, however, as a practice it can be incorporated in other, more personal, capacities. Here, we will use the premise of the intent behind what it means to do due diligence in order to achieve resilience. Simply stated, due diligence is a thorough and considerate approach to gathering appropriate information before making a decision.

For example, if you are buying a house, you will want to learn more about the house itself and do an inspection, just as you will want to learn about the neighborhood and community. By researching and gathering this data, you will be able to make a better (stronger, healthier) decision.

When it comes to building resilience, embracing due diligence is a necessary step. It's what allows your mind to shift from one that is externally-focused to one that is internally-aligned. This is not to say that the internal-alignment is one that is self-centered or egotistical and narcissistic. Those are unhealthy approaches to life for a person and everyone around them (and have nothing to do with resilience).

"It's your reaction to adversity, not adversity itself that determines how your life's story will develop."

– Dieter F. Uchtdorf –

No, an internally-aligned mind is about reconnecting to yourself in a way that allows you to truly get to know who you are, what makes you tick, and how you want to show up in the world.

As an example, this would be a shift from wanting to wear the latest fashion trend even though you genuinely don't like it (external focus), to one where you acknowledge the latest fashion trend exists, while still honoring your inner truth and not adopting it (inner alignment), or making aspects of it your own. In other words, if you don't want to wear a belt bag (aka: bum bag, fanny pack) across your chest, you don't have to. More importantly, you feel good about your decision, because it came from inside you, rather than as an emotional reaction to something external. This is a form of resilience.

By connecting with who you are inside and forging those bonds through inner work (due diligence), you learn more about yourself. This is what provides you with the foundational footing you need to build resilience.

So, if you think resilience sort of just "happens" – it doesn't. Although it may be true that some people look back on their life and suddenly realize they are resilient, the change didn't happen overnight. Even though the realization that you are resilient may feel sudden, the actual work to create resilience always involves a measure of time and effort.

Empowerment vs. Power

> *"I can be changed by what happens to me. But I refuse to be reduced by it."*
>
> — Maya Angelou —

In addition to requiring due diligence to shift your mind, you also need to understand the difference between empowerment and power. This is similar to the previous section's focus on internal alignment and external focus, with an added perspective around intent and action.

When we talk about both power and empowerment, there is an unspoken piece: Outcome. Typically, both power and empowerment have a desired outcome attached to them. This is the identified (and sometimes unidentified) intent inherent in the action.

When aligned with power, the desired outcome is often one that serves to reinforce the power, even if it does something else along the way. The same can be said about empowerment. Empowerment's desired outcome is to generate more empowerment. There is, however, a major difference between the two, and that is their fuel requirement.

Unlike empowerment, power requires a constant fuel source. It must always be fed in order to stay relevant. Empowerment, on the other hand, exists once it is created. Even though acts of empowerment serve to reinforce it, if there are no future acts of empowerment, it still remains. The same cannot be said for power. Power, as a construct, is fleeting and requires constant maintenance. For examples, look to the greatest use of power in the world: dictatorships and authoritarian regimes.

> *"A good half of the art of living is resilience."*
>
> — Alain de Botton —

They continually need to engage in power struggles in order to exert their power and prove they still have it. They often create power struggles just for this purpose. Power is an externally-focused initiative. It must always look outside itself in order to exist. It has to have something to push against in order to feel true, or be considered valid or real.

Conversely, empowerment is internally-aligned. Once it has been created, it stays. It may go quiet or dormant for a while as circumstances change, but if you need it, it's there.

You can always call on it once it's created. It never needs an ongoing fuel source, though it can be reinforced by engaging in more empowering actions. As such, empowerment is a bedfellow of resilience, whereas power is not.

Even though both empowerment and power can appear to be about strength, when it comes to resilience, only one is truly strong because it's lasting. Just like empowerment, resilience is lasting. Once you have created it, it's there.

It can build on itself, but it never goes away. Not really. It may go dormant or feel out of reach when situations change or are new, but it's still there, just waiting for you to remember and call on it.

Who Is Most Resilient?

"Resilience is based on compassion for ourselves as well as compassion for others."

— Sharon Salzberg —

Everyone has some measure of resilience within them. As children, we are taught how to stumble, fall, and try again. This is how most infants turn into toddlers (and why we call them toddlers—because they toddle). To toddle is to take short unsteady steps while learning to walk. The key word in all of that is: Learning.

Learning builds resilience.

Yes, it really is that simple. As long as you are open to learning, you can build resilience. This also means that everybody is resilient on some level. So, who is most resilient? Before we dive into that, we need to start with a bit of a qualifier.

Don't Put People On Pedestals

In our aspirational culture, we have a tendency to put people on pedestals. We do this because they have something we want, or think we want (because we're told we should want it). These individuals have something we think we can't have, something that often feels out of reach or unattainable.

This is what makes it aspirational. When something feels aspirational, our response is often to put that person (and/or the quality) on a pedestal—forever keeping it out of reach and above us. But it bears noting that <u>we</u> are the ones doing that.

Even if someone wants to be on a pedestal in relation to our lives, only we can actually put them there. If we choose not to see them on a pedestal, they aren't.

The same applies for qualities that people display. If, for example, you put resilience on a pedestal, you are the one that is making it seem out of reach, not the resilient person.

Therefore, in order to talk about the people who are most resilient, we must first understand that nobody is on a pedestal, nor should they be. Their life is different (not better or worse) than others' lives, and as a result, they have built more resilience.

In general, the people who are most resilient are the ones that have been willing to show up at their most vulnerable and have been humble enough to learn. They have been curious enough to engage with life in a different way and have been open enough to accept wisdom from others.

The people who are most resilient are those that have made a choice to become the best versions of themselves. Simultaneously, they also understand that the best version is always part of a process of evolution and growth—and always a continual work in progress.

For some, this process can take a lot of time and involve a fair amount of hardship and struggle. For others, it can seem easier or smoother, involving less struggle, but more challenges. For both, it always includes a measure of humility, curiosity, and willingness. If, for example, you are unable to be humble and curious (you think you're "right"), you will not build resilience. Similarly, if you are looking to blame others, then you are not willing to engage differently and will not build resilience. Resilience is a byproduct of growth, and as such, it requires you to check your ego at the door so that you can actually learn and evolve.

The most resilient among us have learned this, often the hard way.

When someone says "I want to be like you" to someone who is very resilient, it's highly likely that the resilient person is saying in their head, "be careful what you wish for" because they know that their resilience was hard-won.

> *"My scars remind me that I did indeed survive my deepest wounds. That in itself is an accomplishment. And they bring to mind something else, too. They remind me that the damage life has inflicted on me has, in many places, left me stronger and more resilient. What hurt me in the past has actually made me better equipped to face the present."*
>
> *– Steve Goodier –*

We are all, always, in a state of becoming; who you choose to become is up to you. How you choose to engage is up to you. A more resilient person understands this and focuses on both the long-game and the present at the same time. They know that life is much more than just this moment, and simultaneously, they know how they want to show up in the moment itself.

Nobody suddenly becomes the best version of themselves, nor is a "best version" something to be achieved. The more accurate phrase is to be the best version of yourself, for now. For today. For this moment. This means that you have left room for an even better version tomorrow, or in the next moment.

A resilient person understands that they are always growing, while still enjoying who they have become and appreciating all the work they have already put in to get there. A person who desires to be resilient, but isn't willing to do the work will end up in a constant cycle of chasing resilience, which ultimately actually undermines any resilience they already had.

Chasing resilience is a resilience-killer.

It chips away at whatever resilience is already there, because it goes against the truth that it's a byproduct of other work; by making resilience the focus (which is externally-driven), you are actually redefining what resilience is and thereby removing any resilience you had by reclassifying it.

Resilience needs to be an internal process and there is nobody whose life you can compare your own to to then be able to go learn their lessons and become resilient yourself. You have to do it based on your own life, your own life experiences, your own mind, your own heart, your own body and your own soul. It cannot be done by adopting somebody else's work, tools, or exercises.

When Do We Need Resilience Most?

"We must be willing to let go of the life we planned so as to have the life that is waiting for us."

— Joseph Campbell —

We need resilience most in our daily life. A lot of people think that we need resilience the most when we are in crisis, but that's not true. In a crisis, we can draw on other resources (including resilience) to help us get through, but in everyday life, resilience is one of our primary tools, if not the primary tool we use.

Think about it this way: In your everyday life, there are certain things you do that are both for the present moment as well as the long run. For example, brushing your teeth is something that serves you now (your teeth are clean and your mouth and breath are fresh), and later (you prevent cavities and other issues). Brushing your teeth is like building resilience; it serves you both today and in the long-run. It serves you by being consistent over time, as well as being flexible in how you allow it to evolve. Most of us have changed the way we brush our teeth from when we were children, for example.

It's this flexibility that is what makes resilience so important in our daily lives. It is what allows us to navigate annoying situations with more ease, staying grounded in who we are. This looks like the person in line at the store who seems to be unphased by the cashier chatting with the other customers in front of them. In truth, unless you are a first responder and there is an emergency, there is no reason to get frustrated by someone taking an extra 15-30 seconds to enjoy a conversation. Even if it's a minute, it's still not going to really impact anybody's day in a negative way; however, it might improve both the cashier and the customer's day immensely. A more resilient person knows this. They choose to remain calm and happy in themselves white waiting in line.

Conversely, a less resilient person might get more frustrated, start to complain, and try to engage people around them to join in with their complaint. This is because when someone isn't feeling resilient, they move from a place of empowerment to a place of power, and power needs fuel. By engaging people in the complaint, the less resilient person has acquired the fuel he or she needs to continue to complain. And the cycle continues, keeping the person out of opportunity for growth, and out of opportunity for building resilience.

This is why we need more resilience in our daily lives than when we are in crisis, tragedy, or trauma. The truth of the matter is that it's the daily struggles we encounter as humans that wear us down and erode our will and well-being over time. By necessity, resilience really comes into play when you are navigating life's daily obstacles that serve to undermine the higher frequency emotions of hope, love, joy, or peace.

What About Trauma And Tragedy?

"Although the world is full of suffering, it is also full of the overcoming of it."

— Helen Keller —

Though resilience is part of the equation, trauma, tragedy, and crisis will always require a layer of strength that we don't regularly—and shouldn't need to—access in our daily life. These extenuating circumstances are born of something extreme or egregious. If they are part of your daily life, then that is a totally different situation. In those instances, we are talking about a particular form of resilience that is being built, one that includes fortitude and tenacity, and is more about survival than resilience.

When it comes to a crisis, however, you rarely get through it by being resilient. In other words, resilience alone is not enough to get through tragedy.

Instead, most people initially get through those things by being resourceful or strong; they have an adrenaline rush that helps them manage the situation in order to get to the other side—to where the crisis can abate and things can revert in some way back to "normal."

Once a new normal is created, resilience is back at the helm helping the person create new ways to navigate daily life.

When it comes to resilience, it's best and most often used in daily life. It helps us make our daily existence easier and better; it also helps to create more opportunities for us to experience higher frequency emotions. Resilience is required to maintain some measure of inner peace. It is required to maintain a belief in hope, love, and joy. Therefore, we need resilience the most on a daily basis.

> *"Our greatest glory is not in never falling, but in rising every time we fall."*
>
> — Confucius —

As we have already discussed, resilience is not something you can learn in a book, a meditation, or a yoga class. Nor is it something you can acquire by listening to others, such as in podcasts or webinars. Resilience is—and always will be—an inside job.

That being said, it is possible to learn about resilience (what it means and what it might feel like) by reading a book or listening to someone's story. This can help you better recognize it when you are undergoing it or experiencing it, which can then help you make decisions that reinforce it. But, in order to truly learn resilience and grow your own resilience, it has to be done in the little day-to-day things that help support you in your well-being and on your soul's path and journey.

What are these little things?

They are the daily decisions you make in your life that offer you opportunities to shift your thinking and your perspective.

To use an earlier example: Consider your most mundane activities, such as grocery shopping. Now, think about the last time you were frustrated in the check-out line because something was happening outside your control.

In that moment—that very real, very simple moment—you had a choice. You could either get frustrated and ramp up your low frequency emotions, or you could take a breath and choose to occupy your mind in a different, healthier way.

Which did you choose? And what was the result? If you chose to ramp up, what could you do differently next time to make a different choice? If you chose to occupy your mind, how else could you occupy your mind that feels even more aligned with your well-being? (Could you read a funny text or meme instead of checking in on work emails, for example?)

Building resilience is all about the little choices we make on a daily basis and how we learn from them. If you're not willing to learn, you can't gain resilience. More importantly, perhaps, if you don't see those small events as opportunities to learn, you will be making this much harder than it needs to be.

If you can't see these opportunities through the lens of learning, how about seeing them as remembering? It's true that sometimes we don't want to see something as a learning opportunity because it triggers us. When we feel triggered, most opportunities are off the table. But there's another way...

"No matter how bleak or menacing a situation may appear, it does not entirely own us. It can't take away our freedom to respond, our power to take action."

– Ryder Carroll –

Remembering is a tool you can use to take some of the triggers out of a situation that is "pinging" you. It can then put you back into a space where you can recognize that you are more empowered than you thought.

What kind of remembering does this? Remembering that you have a choice.

This is a big step toward increasing your resilience. Many people forget that they have a choice in most situations. Remembering that single truth can help build your resilience from the inside out. Focusing on choice helps you show up differently, and showing up differently builds your resilience because you can apply the process more easily the next time.

Resilience is something that you learn through practice. That is why you can't just learn resilience from reading, taking a class, or listening to someone. It requires your engagement and a willingness to connect with yourself in new ways. Remembering is a tool that can help you get there.

There's another aspect of remembering that's also important when it comes to building resilience, but to understand it, we need to juxtapose it with holding on.

"If your heart is broken, make art with the pieces."

– Shane Koyczan –

Holding and Remembering

When we hold onto something, we are preventing it from moving through. For example, when you hold onto a previous version of a person (perhaps a memory from high school), you are limiting yourself and keeping yourself trapped in that version of events.

You can't build resilience when you're stuck. To hold onto a grudge is to keep yourself stuck. More so, the other person is probably not stuck, which means that you are now the victim of your own actions, not theirs.

Holding on requires memory, but not in the good way—not in the way we previously discussed. Holding onto a narrative, a thought, a belief, is akin to cementing those items in your psyche, which will never allow for the mental flexibility required to grow resilience.

"Forgive yourself for your faults and your mistakes and move on."

— Les Brown —

> *"Persistence and resilience only come from having been given the chance to work through difficult problems."*
>
> — Gever Tulley —

As we know, resilience is an inside job, and holding onto something outside of yourself directly contradicts that.

Conversely, remembering (without holding on) can be incredibly helpful in building resilience. You can let the memory of an event inform you as you let the triggers go.

With the information, you are now free to make different choices—choices that support you in building resilience. Memory becomes a tool to support your inner growth, because you are using it to gather data, or evidence, or what you do or don't want in your life.

As a tool, memory provides you with information. Nothing more and nothing less. If you attach emotions to the memories, you might be holding on and keeping yourself out of the potential for more resilience.

Why Do We Need To Focus On Resilience?

*"My barn having burned down,
I can now see the moon."*

— Mizuta Masahide —

We need to focus on resilience for all of the reasons we've already discussed, but also because our soul wants us to evolve. We want to evolve; it's our natural state of being. We are not talking about evolving just physically and biologically as a human race or as a planet or a species, though those are all good reasons. It's more than that. We are hard-wired for growth, so much so that it's an inherent desire.

As a species, we don't do well when things are stagnant. Though we like the security and stability of routine, we also accept that change is one of the constants of the human condition, just as it is a constant of the universe. One of the easiest ways to embrace change is to do so from a stable, but flexible, place. This is the epitome of resilience.

Focusing on resilience is what allows us to see where we are deficient, which translates to: Where can I still learn? For example, if you find yourself easily upset from small inconveniences, this is a place you can focus on to grow and evolve.

Similarly, if you find yourself constantly checking social media for fear of missing out on something, this is a place where you can grow and evolve. The best way to assess where you have opportunities to grow in resilience is to identify the things that are 1) external to you and outside of your control, and 2) cause you stress.

If you are feeling stress from situations that have little to do with you or your internal life, you can see those as learning opportunities, or opportunities where you can increase your understanding and resilience. They are opportunities for you to learn new tools that can help you find more inner peace in the long run.

That's resilience.

"No matter how much falls on us, we keep plowing ahead. That's the only way to keep the roads clear."

– Greg Kincaid –

Slightly different are the opportunities that are still external but actually have something to do with your internal life. Though they are still opportunities, they can be a bit harder to learn within. If you think of the opportunities mentioned above as grade-school-level, then these new opportunities would be more like college-level.

They are still external to you (meaning you don't control them), but because they affect you internally, they require more skill, patience, and practice. They are not the check-out line scenarios, but might be more like watching a friend make choices you know will hurt them, and not being able to do anything about it.

This is why we need to focus on resilience as something to include in our overall sense of well-being.

"Enthusiasm is common. Endurance is rare."

– Angela Duckworth –

By including resilience in the conversation, even though we cannot pursue it directly, we open the door to converting previously frustrating situations into something we can use to grow and evolve... through the lens of building resilience.

Doing so helps us evolve in a more stable, kind, and compassionate way than if we were to just stumble through everything all the time, keeping things at arm's length. One of the best ways to stay aligned with who we are (as well as the higher frequency emotions that feel good) is to be resilient.

Resilience helps us evolve, and it does so by making our evolution more rewarding along the way.

How Do We Build Resilience?

"I knew exactly what kind of effort I was going to need to get where I wanted to go."

— *Vernon Davis* —

By now, you understand that resilience is not something you can set as a goal and take direct steps to achieve. Though you can think of it as something you want to build, you will need to take action on other goals in order to get there. Simply stated, you can't make a "to do" list for building resilience in the same way that you can make a list of things to do to lose ten pounds or train for a marathon. It's simply not tangible in the same way.

The good news about this is that resilience is a side effect or byproduct of taking action on many other things. It grows as a result of your commitment to engaging in life, which means your opportunities for creating more resilience are almost endless. The one variable you don't control, however, is time. And time is definitely part of the equation.

Resilience and Time

As with all things that are worth the wait, resilience takes time. It takes time to build the habits that create the opportunities for you to make different decisions.

If we go back to the idea of standing in a check-out line, you will need to do this multiple (probably many) times before you really start to notice a change in your resilience. It could take weeks, months or years, and in truth, it will probably always be evolving.

> *"Resilience is very different than being numb. Resilience means you experience, you feel, you fail, you hurt. You fall. But, you keep going."*
>
> — Yasmin Mogahed —

When you make time your ally in any situation, you have unlocked a superpower. In today's culture where attention is a commodity and speed is a reward, time suddenly becomes a valuable asset. Or rather, the allowance for time becomes a valuable asset. If you are not buying into the hustle and rush that is probably flowing all around you, you are removing the externalized stimulus that is likely to chip away at your resilience most easily.

Finding Strength In The Midst Of Struggle

Another part of the equation is perspective. The ability to take perspective is one of the most underestimated tools in people's toolbox. When you can take perspective—truly take perspective—and understand someone else's situation and position, you can make different (often better) choices. This opens up a world of possibility, including the ability to find strength in the midst of struggle.

Taking perspective is akin to being able to think outside of the box. It's a quality that is often cited in situations that require innovation or resourcefulness, but it goes beyond that. The ability to think differently creates a much larger selection of choices for any situation. You are not locked into the prescribed way of being, way of acting, or way of thinking.

This is not only helpful in stressful situations, but can be beneficial in everyday life as well as serve as an example to others.

If you are faced with a screaming child in a shopping cart, and you choose to react differently, by engaging with it in a playful way, not only will you be showing the people behind you that another choice is possible, you will be helping the child, too.

By behaving differently and modeling resilience, you give other people permission to make a different choice in the future as well. In a world where everyone is trying to fit in and feel a sense of belonging, that is a superpower, indeed. We are more likely to work on our own resilience when we see it modeled in others around us.

> *"Resilience isn't a single skill. It's a variety of skills and coping mechanisms."*
>
> *– Jean Chatzky –*

Resilience Is Not The Same As Resistant

Resilience is not about weakness or strength; it's more than that. Resilience is about having tools and knowing when and how to use them. It's not about resisting life around you, or rejecting a narrative that's presented to you.

It's about recognizing and acknowledging life and its narratives and owning that you get to choose how you are going to show up. You are going to choose how you let life affect you.

For example, you may not be able to control the weather, but you get to choose whether you are going to enjoy it, stay neutral about it, or condemn it.

For some, resisting the status quo can feel like a form of resilience, but that's usually more about power than empowerment, because it's still related to something externalized to you. Plus, to do it in a way that is 100% about resilience would almost require a PhD in understanding resilience. The majority of people don't have that degree. Instead, if you can keep the line between internal and external clear, you have a greater chance of aligning with building resilience than reacting to an external stimulus.

For some, resisting the status quo can feel like a form of resilience, but that's usually more about power than empowerment, because it's still related to something externalized to you. Plus, to do it in a way that is 100% about resilience would almost require a PhD in understanding resilience. The majority of people don't have that degree. Instead, if you can keep the line between internal and external clear, you have a greater chance of aligning with building resilience than reacting to an external stimulus.

Ultimately, building resilience takes three things:

- Thoughtful engagement with life
- Alignment with empowerment instead of power
- Discernment in understanding what is external vs. internal

If you can keep this focus in all your daily activities and make choices that are aligned with your internal world, you can steadily build resilience. There is no inherent need for hardship and struggle to create resilience, though it is true that many do develop it that way.

What's more true is that simply living your daily life as a human on earth creates ample opportunities for you to increase your resilience. When you realize this, the result is a more empowered presence, which can ultimately lead to more resilience.

"No one escapes pain, fear, and suffering. Yet from pain can come wisdom, from fear can come courage, from suffering can come strength — if we have the virtue of resilience."

— Eric Greitens —

Conclusion

When we talk about resilience, either a willow tree or a palm tree are often used to describe what it means in a somewhat tangible way. This is because both of these trees are fixed and flexible. They can withstand incredible winds and storms, while still staying rooted to the ground.

In many ways, they are the perfect metaphor for resilience. They embody the simplest definition that we often come up with, especially when looking back in hindsight: Resilience is the result of a life lived through hardship and struggle.

Through the hardship of storms—through the high winds and pelting rains— these trees are living. They are still alive, still standing, and still living. It's also true, however, that they are living through all the days that aren't stormy, that aren't rough.

They live through the days that are sunny and overcast, just as they live through the days that are filled with birds and bees buzzing about. Given the ratio of stormy days to non-stormy days, it's safe to say that they live a majority of their time through life's daily ins and outs.

Willows and palm trees live through life, just as we do. Their resilience allows them to stay grounded when things get tough, but also allows them to stay grounded when things "seem" easy. For all we know, they could be fighting off a fungal disease deep beneath the surface that we don't see.

Like us, they use their resilience every day, building on it and expanding it.

We can do the same.

(continued...)

In everything we do, and everything we experience, we can build resilience. In everyday situations, this can look like having the ability to pause before speaking, or choosing not to engage with someone who is acting out until they have calmed down.

It can also look like making a choice not to engage in gossip or making assumptions about something or someone without asking.

However resilience shows up for you, the simplest truth is that every opportunity you have to make a decision has the potential to build resilience, and you get to make those choices.

"The oak fought the wind and was broken, the willow bent when it must and survived."

— Robert Jordan —

"The quality of your life is based on the choices you make."

– Martina E. Faulkner –

About the Author

Martina E. Faulkner is a cross-genre author whose work focuses primarily on exploring what it means to be human, both the unique and the universal. She holds a trifecta in the mental health/healing world as a therapist, certified life coach, and Reiki Master Teacher. This distinctive background allows her to draw on her professional and personal experience in her writing, whether fiction, nonfiction, or poetry.

A self-proclaimed Anglophile, Martina drinks tea daily, loves walks in nature, and enjoys looking at beautiful images from the British Isles while dreaming up her next book. You can read her regular column ('Unique and Universal') on Substack, follow her on Instagram and Facebook @martinaefaulkner, or visit martinaefaulkner.com.

As a children's author Martina's debut children's book, <u>When the World Went Quiet</u>, was given as a gift to Sir David Attenborough, who referred to it as "charming."

Other Books

Understanding Gratitude
Understanding Grief
Understanding Karma
50 and F*ck It!
What if..?
Love and Pain
Infinite In My Heart
Me: 365
The Author's Journey
Crafting the Perfect College Essay

Children's Books

When the World Went Quiet
Princess Wigglebottom and the Forgotten Christmas

www.ingramcontent.com/pod-product-compliance
Lightning Source LLC
Chambersburg PA
CBHW041436120626
46547CB00002B/241